# *The* HANDMADE GRIMOIRE

## A creative treasury for magickal journalling

LAURA DERBYSHIRE

DAVID & CHARLES

www.davidandcharles.com

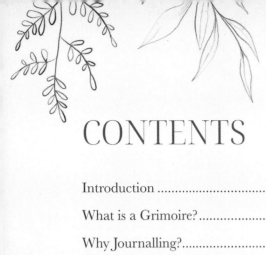

# CONTENTS

I felt that I could capture that joyful creative essence, and combine it with my witchcraft journey

# INTRODUCTION

It may be wrong of me to make any assumptions, but if you've picked up this book, I imagine that you:

*a) are a witch*
*b) enjoy journalling*
*c) both of the above.*

I also assume that you take a lot of joy from the beautiful, tactile elements attached to journalling. Kaleidoscopic inks, floral stamps, patterned papers and translucent stickers make creating artistic journals one of the most joyful forms of self-expression.

Welcome! You are in excellent company here as I adore this form of journalling and all that comes with it.

When I was little, nothing delighted me more than interactive books, the ones where you would be encouraged to lift flaps, pull tabs, turn cogs and peep through windows. You may be familiar with the children's book *The Jolly Pocket Postman*, if not it was a rather marvellous book in which the reader follows a postman around on his delivery route. I was obsessed with it growing up as it was stuffed with envelopes containing letters, smaller books, puzzles and other wonderful trinkets. It was such an inspiration to me that I began to make my own versions of tiny books and leaflets. My bedroom became a veritable 'badger sett' of torn-up paper and scattered pens, a hub of creative activity that I would carry with me into my adult life.

At the time I was too little to realise that this was an activity that would feature heavily in my work as a witch. When I first dipped my toes into the rushing waters of witchcraft, it was my creativity that kept me from being swept away in the torrents of information that can sometimes make a beginner witch flounder. There was so much to take in, so many different paths, beliefs and opinions and as I practiced spells, learned tarot, and dutifully followed rituals, I penned my experiences in notebooks. These notebooks were filled with pages and pages of writing, but any time I returned to them to look up a particular ingredient, I felt bored by them.

5

## From notebooks to creativity

It was when I thought back to those moments as a little girl, sitting at the dining room table with my safety scissors, bright yellow card and scented felt tips, that I felt that I could capture that joyful creative essence, and combine it with my witchcraft journey. So I started decorating my grimoires, very basically at first – a sticker here and a highlighter there – but soon I was creating extra fold-out pages, envelopes, and flaps that could be lifted to reveal more information. I was having an absolute blast and what was once a chore, dutifully done but not enjoyed, was now play.

During 2020's pandemic-related winter lockdown I decided to create my most ambitious grimoire yet, using a 500-page plain notebook that I would stuff with all my witchy knowledge and create amazing pages in. I shared this process online and people were delighted and inspired. This led to me sharing more tips and tricks with my growing community of online followers, as well as challenging myself to create even more magickal spreads.

That enormous grimoire has since disintegrated, its spine weakened and split from being stuffed with so much knowledge (and card, glue, string, stickers etc), but it taught me so much about what materials to use, what to avoid, what thickness of paper will tolerate paint and pen, and how to thread ribbon between pages. I will keep it to take inspiration from, but I am ready to start a new grimoire, one that can tolerate a bit more chaotic creativity, and I would love to take you along on the journey of creating it.

## Let's make a new grimoire!

The aim of this book is firstly to show you how creating a grimoire is just as much a part of your craft as rituals and spells. I'll talk about what a grimoire is and what is included within its pages. We'll discuss the benefits that taking time to create your own magickal book can bring, including greater insight into your craft and better mental health through mindfulness. I will walk you through the best way to get stuck in and share the secrets behind ageing paper, creating envelopes and adding unique elements to your spreads.

In the following pages I will offer gentle advice and encouragement to help you get the most out of your creativity and bring some childlike joy to the way that you approach creating spreads. We'll talk about how to cultivate a magpie mind – the act of gathering supplies from the things you have in your home rather than spending a lot of money on new materials. I'll include instructions on how to make your own sigils to keep your grimoire safe and how you can include it in rituals to infuse it with different energies.

I'll be creating and updating my new grimoire as we go through this book, and I hope that you'll join me on the journey. Remember that your creativity is unique. My spreads are meant to inspire, but of course you can create whatever you like and I encourage you to delve deep into your imagination. My tips and tricks will bolster your own ingenuity, and it is my greatest wish that you end up with a tome that you not only created from scratch but take joy from every time you open it.

**WHAT ARE SPREADS?**

You will see me use the term 'spread' a lot in this book. I'm referring to the name we journal-fans give to a decorated page, which can mean just a single page but more usually refers to a double page, and it gives a name to a finished project, or one you are working on. Spreads are the pages in their decorative form: organised and laid out in whichever order is convenient, accessible and memorable to you.

8

Remember that
your creativity
is unique

# WHAT IS A GRIMOIRE?

Is there more to a grimoire than just this definition?
Where did they come from? Who were they for?
What place do they have in today's modern witchcraft?
Is a grimoire the same thing as a book of shadows?

# grimoire

/grɪmˈwɑː/

noun: grimoire; plural noun: grimoires

a book of magic spells and invocations.

*The Oxford English Dictionary*

Historically, grimoires first made their appearance in ancient Mesopotamia and their presence is recorded in every era and culture, starting with the Greeks and Romans, the Egyptians, all the way through the Early Modern Period, and up to today. Their meanings and subject matter have varied depending on their author, audience and religious spectrums, but the consensus is that a grimoire contains spells, magickal or mystical information, guidance and rituals, so it takes the form of a magickal encyclopaedia. Grimoires weren't only to be found in Paganism; they also made an appearance in Abrahamic religions. These texts contained medicinal information as well as divination, demonology and alchemy. They were used by magickal practitioners – those with seemingly 'higher' knowledge from the Gods – who catalogued their divine information into texts that varied in design, from vellum bound tomes to dusty scrolls hidden in the crevices of desert caves.

The history of grimoires is a vast one, spanning ages and cultures, and to cover it all would take an entire book. For more information, I would recommend historian Owen Davies' marvellous manuscript, *Grimoires: A History of Magic Books.*

In modern times we see the grimoire featured in media such as TV and books: look no further than the popular television programs about vampire slayers and witches, and in the literary works of HP Lovecraft. Seeing these magickal books in popular culture evokes a feeling of curiosity, and I remember as a child yearning for leatherbound books and journals full of arcane knowledge. There was something about seeing illustrations, such as dried plants and fountain pen ink scrawled on crumpled ivory pages, that ignited a creative spark in me and made me want to make a tome of my own.

Originally, I wanted to create journals that wouldn't have looked out of place as props in a movie, but my natural progression from 'nosy, feral, nature-child' to witch allowed these artsy journals to transform into something I could not only create but something I could also use in my craft.

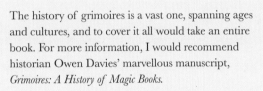

The rising popularity of witchcraft and neopaganism in today's social media-driven society means that grimoires have escaped from the dusty shelves of old libraries and have taken on a new and more personal form, one that finds itself very much at home in the creative community. Just searching for the word 'grimoire' on online image-sharing services, floods your screen with beautifully curated books full of decorated pages, and there seems to be a commonality in what witches find important to document and what they like to share.

A grimoire can take many forms depending on how you practice as a witch. For green witches, it will most likely be filled with botanical knowledge – drawings of plants and spell recipes that contain them. For celestial witches, astronomy and astrology will feature heavily; the moon and her phases and cosmological magick will make an appearance too. If you are eclectic and like to dabble in all aspects of witchcraft then this will be a wonderful tome, full of all the knowledge relevant to you and your practice.

In their most basic form, my own grimoires have acted as containers for all my knowledge as a hedge witch. My refined spells and rituals are lovingly copied into its pages, practical information about herbs intertwines with their magickal meanings, and there are maps and guides for astral travel, and meditative and path-walking exercises. These grimoires would make a good read for other witches, but it is the personal meaning and energy used during their creation that makes them *my* grimoires.

## Grimoire or book of shadows?

You may have heard the term 'book of shadows', and I've often received questions asking if this is the same as a grimoire. There seems to be a general agreement between most witches that they are separate books. As I said before, a grimoire acts as an encyclopaedia of your witchy knowledge, whereas a book of shadows takes a more personal route. It is here that you can keep a journal of your spiritual journey, jot down dreams and what you think they mean, note the happenings of any astral journeys that you have taken, tarot spreads, inner-child healing… The list is extensive, but this book of shadows should be kept entirely to yourself, a secret diary of your innermost spiritual feelings and findings.

Your own vision for your grimoire might look a little different to the spreads in this book, and that's more than okay. Depending on your practice you will want to research some things, become an expert in others and take a little more time on subjects that I may not have mentioned. There is no right way to create something as personal as this sort of book, but there are cunning practicalities that I can show you to add extra space and squeeze in as much information as possible. I can also show you how to infuse your grimoire with intention, invocations, and protective and healing qualities. Just like grimoires of old, this will be a tome to inform as well as enchant.

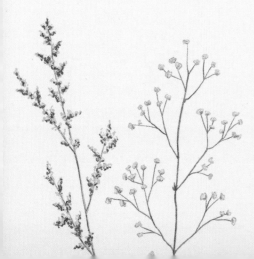

I can show you
how to infuse
your grimoire
with intention,
invocations, and
protective and
healing qualities

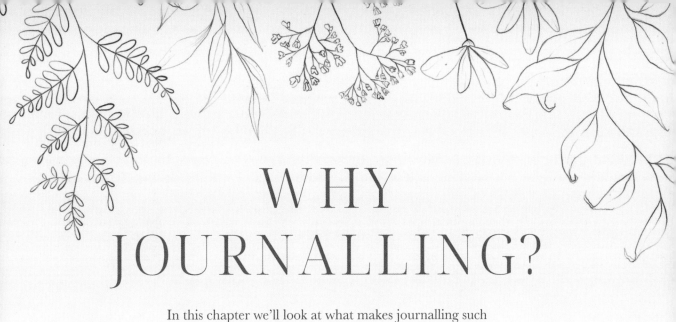

# WHY JOURNALLING?

In this chapter we'll look at what makes journalling such a key part of a self-care routine, and how to incorporate it into your everyday life. We'll look at how to find your own style and why there are much better options than simply keeping a daily diary. And we'll find that all journal styles have something in common: they are an outlet.

# Explore your journalling life

Journalling comes in many shapes and forms, and within its bounds contains a wide range of artistic styles. For some, their journalling practice simply consists of jotting down their thoughts in a minimalist fashion; for others it is an artistic expression that involves a creative flair that would rival most canvases. At the root of it, all these polarised journal styles have something in common: being an outlet.

We are all familiar with the concept of meditation. The idea of sitting with yourself, quietening your mind and allowing yourself to relax and process difficult emotions sounds relatively simple, but I find it very hard to meditate. Switching off and sitting in silence, and training my brain to let go of thoughts, has been an issue for me since I first started to try to master meditation. However, I have found that when I journal or create in my grimoire, I gain the same sort of results that traditional meditation promises.

**WHAT CAN THE BENEFITS BE?**

The cathartic act of writing down your thoughts and freeing them from your brain acts almost like moving data from your computer to an external hard drive. Nothing is destroyed or forgotten, but moving those thoughts elsewhere gives your brain the space to run better, to think more clearly and stop any kind of mental lag that can lead to heightened feelings of frustration and anger.

When you throw art into the mix it creates a wonderful almost trance-inducing state of mind. You are present enough to make sure you don't snip your fingers with your scissors, but relaxed enough to allow your mind to wander, to drift into a daydream and eventually into a place that some like to call 'creative flow'. You may have experienced it before when engrossed in a task like sewing, sketching or colouring – you are so at ease that when you eventually glance at the clock, an hour has passed by in the blink of an eye and you haven't thought about much.

I love the relaxing feeling that journalling offers and as a result I'm a bit of a journal fanatic. I have nature journals stuffed with weekly diary entries about what I've seen on my walks. I have life journals where I create pages on everything from favourite films to foods. There are homemade recipe journals, reading diaries, writing journals and even a classical music journal.

Journalling is a warm comforting space for me, where the meditative benefits of creative seeds are born and their curation results in personal books that I can

# 'Why so many journals? Where on earth do I find the time?'

look back on in years to come. I don't find content merely to have a daily diary, one in which I ritually and dutifully fill out every little aspect of my day. It just doesn't interest or spark any creativity in me. I have also realised, that when writing daily, I often tend to veer towards negative documenting. It is important to vent, to write down your frustrations and get them out of your head, but if you have a run of bad luck or things are generally dreadful, then your daily journalling is going to turn into something miserable.

## WHAT INTERESTS YOU?

I know that I am so much more than my day-to-day existence and I would encourage you to look at all the little interests and genres in your life…

Perhaps you are a keen gardener, if so then I would take those green fingers and plunge them into a journal that is full of your plant knowledge, cut-outs or drawings of your favourite flowers, fictional garden maps and how you would design them, and what plant you would put where. If you have a love for making your own clothes then a sewing diary is a wonderful thing. It can be full of scaled-down versions of the patterns you have used, polaroids of your creations, fabric samples and dream ideas that you hope one day to achieve.

## WHAT'S THE RUSH?

You may think that to have such a wide range of ideas means you would never have the time to make so many different journals, but what's the rush? Journalling is a relaxing process and an act of self-care, just like running a bubble bath or cooking with a glass of wine. Find a little time – between ten minutes to an hour – a few times a week, and you'll soon see the books start to fill. This is a hobby in which to document your hobbies. Don't attempt multiple journals at once (this is a mistake I have made on a few occasions), instead pick a couple of subjects and concentrate on those before you move on to your other ideas. It isn't a race and should be a pastime that continues into your old age, providing you don't run out of ideas!

## Your grimoire:
## so much more than a textbook

Although I have mentioned that a grimoire is more of an encyclopedia than a journal, there are definite similarities in the process of creating them. If I was concerned with just dutifully logging information about my craft then I would probably turn to the sleek minimalism of a digital document and file it away, only opening it when I needed to check something. It is the transformation of textbook to journal that makes a grimoire incredibly special, and the same can be said for any subject that you choose to document in this way, from bird spotting to cake making.

When you take subjects and journal with them, you also make it more likely that your brain will retain the information. Set against the boring act of typing out facts versus creating art around a subject, it's clear that the latter is a much more enjoyable process.

18

It is the transformation of textbook to journal that makes a grimoire incredibly special

# HOW TO BEGIN

You're now familiar with what a grimoire is and why
keeping one is important to your craft, but how on earth
do you begin to create one? Taking the first step in
establishing your grimoire will lead to you growing more
confident, and soon you'll be creating spreads with gusto!

# Choosing your journal

The possibilities for your grimoire are endless, from the type of journal, to selecting your subject matter and style – where on earth do you start? Let's begin by exploring what kind of book your witchy workings should inhabit.

We are spoilt for choice with the many kinds of notebooks, sketchbooks and journals that we have to choose from nowadays but choose you must, and it will be easier to pick if you start by asking yourself a few questions first...

## HOW BIG SHOULD IT BE?

This all depends on what you are wanting to document. If you want to create a general grimoire that has pages on a wide variety of subjects, then you should consider a journal of more than 200 pages. If you want to include a lot of artwork and materials that will need to be glued in, then too many pages will cause the book to swell and eventually warp so that the pages will rip and the spine will disintegrate. Perhaps think about larger dimensions rather than more numerous pages to protect the structure of the book. Folded paper can soon become incredibly thick, so consider how many flaps and hidden doors you want to include too.

## WHAT KIND OF ART STYLE WILL IT BE CREATED IN?

The art materials that you will be using to decorate your pages will probably dictate what sort of journal will be up for the task. Consider page thickness when it comes to what art medium you prefer to work in. Paint and paint pens will require thicker paper, watercolours will most likely need to be painted onto separate watercolour paper and then stuck in. Certain alcohol-based inks are terrible for bleeding through even the thickest of journal paper, so always do a test on a page at the back of your book. With any pen or paint you wish to use, do a little swatch on this test page and look to see how much it bleeds through, if it all. Remember you can always glue pages together that have gone catastrophically wrong, or cover them with patterned paper and start again. Bar the paper tearing, catching fire (believe me, I've done it), getting wet or disintegrating, there isn't much that can't be salvaged when it comes to journalling.

## The cover

They say 'don't judge a book by its cover', but in this case the cover of your grimoire says a lot about you and your craft. Some like their grimoires to be simple and unassuming – an ordinary black cover with no mark or insignia to distinguish it from any other notebook. Others covet beautifully decorated covers that use florals and bright patterns. Some may like to decorate their cover themselves by using stickers, covering it with material, or painting directly onto it. I have done a little of each and the grimoire that features in this book sports a whimsical little forest scene that I painted with a nod to each of the seasons.

Some of you may not want to draw attention to your grimoire. You may not feel safe or comfortable showing parts of your spirituality so openly, but would still really like to create one. Please know that it is perfectly fine to use a normal notebook, such as a ruled jotter or exercise book, one that doesn't offer any clues as to what may be inside.

## The first few pages

The following are just a few ideas for topics for your first few pages and the order they might go in, just to get your own creativity flowing. You can marshal your thoughts into categories like this, or not. Of course, you don't have to arrange them in any particular order, you can be as chaotic or as orderly as you like, and you can mix topics or keep them regimented in separate chapters. It is all part of the creative fun involved in making your grimoire.

### Index/contents

A handy way to keep track of your subjects and to find them easily without thumbing through the entire book.

### Ethos

A little statement about what your ethics and ideals are as a witch, plus the intention of this grimoire and how it will be used. I like to include an ethos page as it is a great reminder of why you started making your grimoire.

### About You

Feel free to include a page about yourself, your craft, your beliefs and possibly your journey into witchcraft or how the idea for this style of grimoire came to you. If you identify as a particular type of witch you could write about what that entails.

### The Wheel of the Year

I like to start with this subject as it is one of the largest and most interesting in terms of research. You can start with a page talking about the significance of this pagan/witch calendar and then move on to each festival. You can create spreads on Yule, Ostara, Imbolc, Litha etc and tie in seasonal elements with each subject, decorating the pages to match the energy of the festival.

### The Elements

Writing about each of the elements and what they represent and are used for can take up quite a bit of space, but each one is incredibly important in the craft so it is a crucial subject. Including pockets in these spreads will give you more room to store information. Use colours that match the elements to add an extra layer of intention to your pages.

*Water = blue hues*
*Air = pastels and whites*
*Fire = reds and oranges*
*Earth = green and brown tones*

### Moon Cycles

Writing about the moon is lovely, so take your time with this spread. You can either draw her phases and write a little about what each one means, or you can make separate spreads on each phase in more detail. Personally, I like to note the phases and then make two separate, detailed pages on the two main phases: the new moon and the full moon. Having a moon journal is a great excuse to create a more niche, specialised grimoire!

### Candle Magick

This is a brilliantly fun spread to make. Write down all the colours of your candles and what their properties are, such as how green is usually associated with prosperity and money, and pink with love and serenity. Note what they are used for and what to combine them with to heighten their magickal energy. I would encourage you to fold in an extra sheet of paper to give yourself a little more space for this large amount of information.

### Cleansing

Make sure to create a page on some basic cleansing rituals and the ingredients you prefer to use. You can look back on these later in your witchy life and see how much your practice has changed and adapted.

### Could you bind your own book?

Bookbinding is a fascinating skill to consider mastering. It is something I have been exploring, and I would love to attempt a grimoire using the tips and tricks I have been learning. The magickal implications of creating your own book from scratch are also alluring. Choosing paper and stitching it together using an intention or incantation for each stitch would be an amazing way to steep the grimoire in magick before it is even used.

It may feel a little daunting, to have so much information ready and waiting to be entered into your book – those blank pages may look a little menacing – but doing a couple of spreads a week will soon produce results. There is nothing jollier than lifting up a journal so plump with knowledge and papers that it can barely shut, and it is a really wonderful feeling to thumb through everything you have accomplished.

## Not being precious

People may think that being artistic means always being happy when creating. Often of course, this is genuinely the case as there is much joy to be found in creative pursuits, but sometimes we are met with a crippling sense of self-consciousness or imposter syndrome. We become so precious about starting that we can't even begin.

### FEAR OF THE BLANK PAGE

It's hard to imagine anything worse as a creator than buying a new sketchbook, opening it at the first page and freezing in fear. You don't want to wreck it; you don't want to feel as though you are wasting supplies, or that you must create something amazing and start this new book as you mean to go on.

This is a fear response: a fear of failing or looking silly, a fear that you're not as good an artist as the artists you admire. You can't bear the thought of having to rip out that first page and feel disappointed… So this one goes on the pile of all the other sketchbooks you haven't filled, and you reach for the 'safe' piece of paper that you feel you can easily dispose of. But it's a flimsy sort of familiar crutch that helps you but doesn't quite allow you to stand on your own.

I imagine that as you've been reading this book you have a sketchbook, journal or notebook in mind that you want to create your grimoire in. You may be feeling daunted at the prospect of writing in its crisp white pages. What if your ink splatters? What if you spell something wrongly? What if your washi tape goes crooked and you lift it up to straighten it but that rips the page? Then what..?

I used to feel like this. I used to covet notebooks and stack them up like priceless first editions, to be looked at and admired but never used. Anytime I plucked up the courage to write in them I would make a mistake and would tear a page out, and it just never felt the same. Seeing those ragged inserts, with binding string hanging out everywhere made me feel guilty and utterly defeated.

### PREPARATION IS KEY

Slowly I started to change how I approached journalling, especially in the making of my grimoire. I used to stare at the blank page, think about what topic I wanted to do a spread on and *then* gather the materials I wanted to decorate it with. I know now that in order to stay relaxed, preparation is key. Having everything measured and cut and ready to stick down saves a lot of hassle if you're feeling in a perfectionist sort of mood. Writing down the facts and information onto another piece of paper, so I could check the spelling and handwriting, and *then* sticking it inside my journal made me feel a lot better than writing directly onto the page. It also stopped ink bleeding through on thinner pages.

### EMBRACE THE SCRAPPY STYLE

As time goes on, you'll start to feel more comfortable about just getting stuck in, and there is so much creativity in mess. Torn pages, stains, ink spills and paint splatters can make a spread look amazing! In fact, some of my favourite pages have been birthed by the spilling of paint or bursting of a fountain pen.

The best part of this messy and scrapbook style of journalling is that things can be layered, resulting in chunky journals that are a jolly sight to behold. There is something so satisfying about feeling the weight of a completed journal in your hands – seeing the ribbons and lace spilling out, and the tufts of paper and material peeking from between the pages. Layering over mistakes, using washi tape to patch up tears, and adding stickers to cover failed attempts at drawing just adds to the character of the book.

Not being precious is a wonderfully freeing gift to bestow upon yourself, so when you glance over at your chosen grimoire vessel, ask yourself if the clinical creation of it will bring you joy, or if you would like to approach it with the wild, unbridled glee you had when you were a child.

Of course, there are spreads that I look at and just am not happy with, and that's fine. I don't destroy them, though sometimes I might pinch a sticker or two to use in a new spread. They are usually just left as a reminder that, even if I'm not always happy with what I've created, at least I created it.

Creativity is a muscle and some workouts are better than others, but to abandon it altogether makes it harder to muster the energy to get back into it. Show up to your workout and flex those creative muscles!

My grimoire
is my magickal
companion,
a sentient
sidekick

# SETTING INTENTIONS

Grimoires are the cornerstone of my practice as a witch,
and this chapter champions their creation. We'll talk about
what makes this seemingly ordinary book of information
into an extraordinary extension of your self-identity and
how you can curate something completely unique to you.

## Its purpose is greater than its parts

The magick of a grimoire is so much more than what is written on its pages. It would be easy to consign it to the role of an encyclopaedia, or a textbook, but doing so does it a grave injustice.

My grimoire is my magickal companion, a sentient sidekick, a lovingly stitched extension of my own identity as a witch, and out of all the tools in my witchy armoury, the grimoire is the one I reach for the most. I have had grimoires in various shapes and sizes, from scraps of paper bundled into a binder, to a digital version on an online image-sharing board. There have been thick leather-bound tomes and slender traveller's notebooks that have all held spells, recipes, rituals, folklore and musings within their ivory-coloured pages. They have been plain, with no decoration save for thin line drawings of sigils and leaves, but now they are elaborate, their creation as much a ritual as any I perform for my craft.

**FROM MUNDANE TO MAGICKAL**

The book on its own is an ordinary, inanimate object. It is through the careful curation, dedication and ritualistic process of creating a grimoire that the mundane turns into the magickal, but just how is this achieved?

'Mundane' describes things in the usual form in which we perceive them. Let's look at an apple as an example: an apple in its ordinary form is a source of food – we can take bites out of it or cut it into slices without thinking too much about it other than its crisp, sweet taste. What makes an apple 'magickal' is when we look at it through the eyes of a witch. Sliced through its equator we notice a five-pointed star in its core, a shape attributed to witchcraft. Suddenly the apple takes on a greater and more spiritual meaning, it is sliced and added to simmer pots to protect and add warmth to a home, it is dried and hung up to absorb negativity from a space. Through the ritual of the witch, the apple becomes magickal.

The same thing applies to your grimoire. When looked at from a mundane perspective we perceive it as a lovely-looking journal, its pages attractively decorated and filled with knowledge. We consign it to being simply an encyclopaedia that's pleasing to the eye. However, when we view it through a magickal lens, the grimoire is transformed into an extension of your spiritual brain. Your lovingly crafted spells and rituals are immortalised within it, and its pages are infused with the energy of your altar or sacred space, and with your own self. It is protected by sigils, charms and paint that is infused with the ash of burnt incantations. There is a sentient and tangible energy that your grimoire gives off, and it is that that makes it more than just a textbook.

That being said, a grimoire should have elements of practicality. There is not much point in making a beautiful book and it not having anything to do with your craft, otherwise it is just an art journal. It is your witchcraft that turns a book into a grimoire, so what sort of practicalities do we need to think of when creating one?

**WHAT WILL YOU INCLUDE?**

If you are someone who identifies as a specific kind of witch (green, hedge, kitchen etc) then that should be the main foundation of your book. As a hedge witch my grimoire features herbs and rituals primarily. It contains spells, incantations and pages on the flora and fauna of my local area. There are recipes for flying ointments and herb bundles to be burned during specific rituals. There is, however, much that I assign to other journals. I have a separate journal for food-related recipes, for example, because the subject is far bigger than a couple of spreads so needs its own space, and its own sigils and rituals surrounding it.

The act of studying, experimenting and then writing down a ritual will help you retain information in a much more enjoyable and positive way than just robotically copying down information from other sources. This also frees up a lot of space in the journal or sketchbook you have dedicated as your grimoire. Space can soon become an issue, so only include the things that feel most important to you, and try not to be too 'wordy'. Sometimes simple step-by-step instructions or an image will suffice.

# The 'need' for a grimoire

You do not have to keep a grimoire to practice witchcraft. It sounds counter-intuitive for me to say so, as the existence of this book relies on you wanting to create one! I will say that it is my firm belief that grimoires are invaluable. Other witches might think that about their wand or their athame, neither of which I use and feel no need to own. It simply comes down to personal preference and practice. But if I had to persuade you, I would stress that putting my grimoires together over the years has been an incredibly rewarding experience both spiritually and mentally. The act of preserving your knowledge, of possibly creating an heirloom for whatever family member or fellow witch you may want to pass it on to when you die, feels like an incredible privilege.

As a hedge witch, I use that name to honour and openly own the title as homage to the witches who came before me, who were women of medicine, healing, midwifery and nature, and who were wrongly persecuted and lost their lives. What they wouldn't have given to have had the liberties that I do, to live where I live in relative safety and to openly be able to practice without fear of death or punishment? If they had been able to create their own grimoire, what knowledge could we have access to now? What secrets would they have been able to tell us, their spiritual descendants?

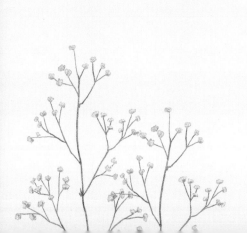

# Connecting to your grimoire

There are ways that you can connect spiritually and energetically to your grimoire, including rituals. The use of sigils throughout your grimoire can be used to enhance and protect it (see Sigils), and some rituals can be done to infuse certain properties into the book itself (as well as the cleansing ritual here, see Rituals later in this book).

### A CLEANSING RITUAL

The first ritual you should do before you start on your grimoire journey is to cleanse the book in which the spreads are going to be created. This can be as simple or as elaborate as you like and can tie in with the usual rituals that you do to cleanse tools or your space.

For new journals, I like to take a highly scented incense such as jasmine or rose, that represents beauty and self-love, and waft it around the cover and in-between the pages of the book. Don't worry if ash falls on the pages and smudges, it adds to the story of the grimoire's creation and doesn't do it any harm. You can always cover it up if you wish. You may also want to sit with your new grimoire for a while and meditate with it on your lap. Visualise how you want it to look, what information you want to put into it and how happy you will be when you finish that last page.

### REFLECT ON YOUR MOTIVATION

If you are like me, you will have dozens and dozens of notebooks that sit in drawers half-finished or not even touched. You may be wondering how on earth you are going to summon the motivation to be able to finish one, especially one that holds so much information. Creating a grimoire also works on your own self-development… you are creating this tome for nobody but yourself. It doesn't need to look anything like anyone else's. It could be that nobody except you will see it – creating something purely for yourself does

wonders for self-esteem, creative play and confidence. With nobody there to judge it, to mark it, to check for spelling errors, or that you are staying inside the line with your colouring, this freedom of expression allows you to unlock a different sort of creative process, one that is cemented in spiritual healing.

### GROW WITH YOUR GRIMOIRE

There is no time restraint when it comes to compiling your grimoire, it does not need to be filled rapidly, it should grow as you do, and growing alongside you will only increase its spiritual strength. Your grimoire will sit at your altar as you crush herbs, fill tinctures and communicate with your ancestors. It will infuse with the unseen energies that are constantly orbiting your sacred space and that emit from you as you practice. When it comes to looking back on spreads you have created, it should not only provide practical knowledge but also inspire you to keep practising your craft. The energy coming from it should feel tangible. Imbuing it with things that delight your senses will make your grimoire feel as though it is a non-furry familiar, a gentle guide and as time goes on, a familiar friend.

The grimoire you make today will most likely not be the same one you are actively using in twenty years from now. You may still possess the worn and tattered original, but it is likely that as you learn, you will outgrow it. You will start new grimoires, in different styles and sizes and on different topics. Some will be basic and others more niche, but it doesn't take away the connection you have to your original grimoire.

# THE ALTAR

A witch's altar is sacred, a space where the veil between worlds is at its thinnest and where spells are practised, potions created and rituals performed. An altar is a place for contemplation and meditation, to read tarot, tea leaves and oracle. It can be a place to communicate with ancestors and deities or it can act as a refuge, a lifeboat in the stormy seas that life sometimes unceremoniously drops us in.

## Creating and curating an altar

Altars can be elaborate, decorated with imagery, trinkets, foraged items and dried flowers, or they can be contained in something as small as a matchbox, pocket-sized and accessible from anywhere. How you develop and curate an altar will entirely depend on what you want to use it for.

My altar is located in my garden studio, it is large and consists of a triangular shelf for all of my crystals, a back wall where I stick imagery and artwork, and a shelf full of animal bones, moss, fossils, totems and runes. It also acts as a place where I can create art and journal, practice spell work and conduct rituals.

### ADAPTABLE SPACES

Altars are adaptable and changeable with the seasons or occasions, and their energy differs greatly throughout the day, the weeks, months and years. I regularly change the imagery on my altar wall. At Samhain it is adorned with pictures of passed loved ones, to honour them and heighten their energy. At Yule I lay out winter foliage like pine, mistletoe and holly to bring in the spirits of that season and enrich the altar with those energies. Ostara sees daffodils and crocus and tealights made from empty eggshells.

### INSPIRATION AND CELEBRATION

The images on my altar bring energy and inspiration to my craft. I am reminded of certain qualities of animals that I wish to invoke – the wisdom of owls or the grace of butterflies; and places that mean a lot to my spirituality, such as Avebury stone circle, a picture of which takes pride of place at the centre of the imagery.

An altar needn't be a testament to anything in particular. Many believe that altars are strictly to venerate gods or ancestors, or other unwordly spirits, and that the imagery and items that adorn them should reflect those beliefs. Of course, people should do what they like at their own altars and decorate them however they feel, but it is important to remember that you can have an altar completely dedicated to yourself. Celebrate yourself amongst all the other things that you believe and that are important to your spirituality. You are the conduit for all of this magickal energy, and your altar should reflect the unique and wonderful being that you are.

## YOUR ALTAR AND YOUR GRIMOIRE

Your altar and your grimoire are energy-wise one and the same. Through imagery, knowledge and your identity as a witch they will end up mirroring each other. The choices you make in your craft will show in the way that your altar and grimoire function. If you are a green witch whose altar is awash with houseplants, and you have dried herbs and a mortar and pestle ready and waiting for your next experiment, there's no doubt that your grimoire will be open and a page about some kind of herb will be visible. Art mirrors life and vice versa, and using this mirroring energy will help tether your identity to these two invaluable commodities in witchcraft. Keep your grimoire close to your altar and see how the two complement each others' energy, looks and content.

The choices you
make in your craft
will show in the way
that your altar and
grimoire function

# CREATIVITY ON THE PAGE

What follows is a treasure chest of pens, paper and artistic paraphernalia that will take your spreads from the mundane to the magickal. In this chapter I will advise you on the types of journals that will work best, what paints to use and what pens to watch out for… who knew there was so much to stationery?!

# Find joy, not guilt, in creativity

Being creative is a unique experience, we all have our own mediums, aesthetics and styles that we like. What one person likes another may wrinkle their nose at, but there is one statement that I believe we can all agree on:

*'Creativity should be playful.'*

For a lucky few of us our creativity is our job, but as a creative millennial I am cursed with the affliction of 'hobby-commodification'. This is the process that starts with picking up a new hobby, then progresses to the realisation that I'm quite good at it, the guilt that comes with taking time out of my schedule to enjoy exploring this new hobby, and then alleviating that guilt by thinking up ideas for how I can turn it into a paying job. Then follows the eventual disinterest and discarding of the hobby because it has turned into work. You may have also experienced this as fellow children of a capitalist society, where we are constantly bombarded with the belief that we can make money through a side hustle away from our '9-to-5'. We're led to believe that we should work twice as hard, and graft when we should be resting. Why on earth should we feel guilt for using our downtime in an enjoyable and relaxing way? It doesn't need to be monetised, it should just be play. When you follow the path of hobby-commodification it leads to hobby abandonments… This is why I also suspect that, like me, you have crochet needles, wood carving tools and felting needles stuffed at the back of a drawer somewhere.

So how can we safeguard the creation of your grimoire from this curse? Journalling and play go hand in hand so let's explore how you can make this hobby exciting and fun…

## PAPERS

I'll be talking more about how to accumulate art supplies in the Cultivating a Magpie Mind section of this book, but for now let's look at how useful papers are in your grimoire.

I often find that the reason I don't want to use a notebook is because I'm worried about writing something wrong, or the ink from the pen ruining the papers. The idea of ripping out a page in a beautiful journal fills me with dread, so instead I tend to write on paper first and then stick it in. That way mistakes can be made and rectified without the need to dissect a perfectly lovely journal.

Papers are a wide-ranging and varied creative asset, you can use decorative ones that come covered in patterns featuring leaves, flowers, birds and animals. You can take plain paper and turn it into a leaf of parchment that looks a hundred years old by tearing it, crumpling it up in your hands, using tea or coffee to stain it or distressing it (cautiously) with a lit match. You can even lovingly create your own – papermaking is a much-enjoyed hobby amongst journal-lovers. My favourite kinds are the ones that are thick and knobbly and peppered with dried wildflowers, so magickal!

## PENS

After many a year of journalling I feel like a bit of a pen *afficionado*. I know what kinds are good for outlining, what to avoid on thin paper, what to use for writing titles, and what to select for the main body of text. The wide choice available may sound complicated, but really you only need a handful in order to create an interesting-looking spread. Here are a few that I can't do without...

**Sakura pens** These technical drawing pens range in nib size from as thin as a cat's whisker to ones that rival bold marker pens, like Sharpies. The variation in these pens is what makes them useful as some days I want to write the tiniest sentence on the smallest slip of paper, and on others I may want to write a big bold title.

**Acrylographs** These are paint pens but they aren't as thick as the ones you usually use for writing on posters. Although they're thin the nibs are tough, and they come in a variety of colours from autumnal hues to spring pastels. I usually use these for line drawings of foliage, or to add interest to borders and paper tags. They sometimes have a habit of leaking so always be ready to whip them away from the page.

**Tombows** These wonderful watercolour-like pens come with blending pens so you can write and then blend colours together. The brush nibs can be tricky to use but with practice the results are lovely. Use for writing titles or for making leafy and floral borders.

## PAINT

You can paint your own subject matter and include it in your book. I like to paint British flora and fauna using a mixture of gouache, watercolour and coloured pencil. It feels incredibly special to see artwork that you have created adorn the pages of your own book. But do not feel discouraged if you perhaps cannot paint as well as you would like, you can still use paint to decorate your grimoire.

Combining paint and collage is the easiest way to get all those gorgeous watercolour-type aesthetics into your pages without feeling as though you are artistically challenged. Abstract art is very forgiving and watercolour even more so. In the Ideas for Inside section of this book, I'll show you how to create a fun collage scene using abstract watercolours.

You do not have to be an amazing illustrator or artist to make beautiful artwork, just by using colour and trusting the medium you are working with, you can create spreads that you love and that inspire you.

## STAMPS

When I first started collecting stationery supplies I always assumed that stamps were just rather blobby looking shapes or words mounted on to wooden blocks. I barely looked at the ones in my local craft shop as they usually featured Rudolph the red nose reindeer, or the words 'happy birthday' or 'with sympathy'. It wasn't until I was enjoying a scroll through Esty, the online craft marketplace, that I saw a lovely little black bird stamp. Intrigued I purchased it only to find that it had arrived as a little rubber cut out and I would need to buy an acrylic block to stick it to. Now I am converted, I have a tin full of stamps that range from caterpillars to swans, blackberries to glass bottles, and spiders to daffodils. All of these can be peeled, stuck and unpeeled from my acrylic blocks and the thrill I get from lifting them to reveal a piece of stamped artwork underneath is marvellous.

If you aren't technically good at drawing I encourage you to invest in these kinds of stamps as they will add an illustrative feel to your grimoire pages, and any other paper projects that you create.

## TACTILITY

My favourite kind of journal spread is one that is not only beautiful to look at, but is also lovely to touch. Ribbons, lace, fabric, string, crumpled paper and scribbled oil pastels make a spread that you can run your fingers over and feel the time and love that has gone into the pages – it's a wonderful thing! However, adding all these elements to your grimoire can make it a little chunky. I've had some trial-and-error when it comes to spines breaking on journals, so bear that in mind when you are deciding what to put on your page. If you can, save material for the borders on the edge of the pages. Opt for thin material and make sure that, if caught, whatever you're sticking in can't damage your pages or book.

Make your grimoire as interactive as you can, add flaps, slides, wheels and things that you have to explore in order to get extra information. The experience makes using your grimoire all the more enjoyable!

You don't
have to be an
amazing artist
to make
amazing art

# IDEAS FOR INSIDE

There are so many wonderful ways to decorate your grimoire, and hopefully you have been inspired by what you've seen in this book. That being said, I have a couple of tips and tricks up my sleeve in order to make the most of your titles. I'll show you how to create beautiful artwork without much technical skill, and how to make your pages interactive as well as lovely to look at.

# HOW TO MAKE
# AN ENVELOPE

These handy little envelopes can be made to whatever size you like, without the use of a template. They are great for holding additional information that won't fit on your page, or acting as a focal point for a spread. If you're using patterned paper decide which side you would like to be on the outside/inside before folding.

**1.** Start with a square of paper or card and fold each half diagonally to its opposite corner. Repeat with both halves and then open out the paper to reveal a crease in the shape of a cross.

**2.** Take one of the corners and fold it into the centre of the cross, and repeat with the opposite side.

**3.** Fold the bottom corner upwards until it meets the top crease line of the original cross. The triangle above it is the top of the envelope.

**4.** Fold the tip of the bottom triangle down to create a crease.

**5.** Open out the bottom triangle and reverse the crease in the tip so it folds inwards.

**6.** Fold the bottom triangle back into place. Glue down the edges, making sure to leave a gap inside where your notes can sit, and then fold the top triangle over to 'close' your envelope.

You can leave the envelope open, or glue it shut to keep the contents safe. The envelope can be attached to your spread via its back, and can be decorated to blend in with the design of your page.

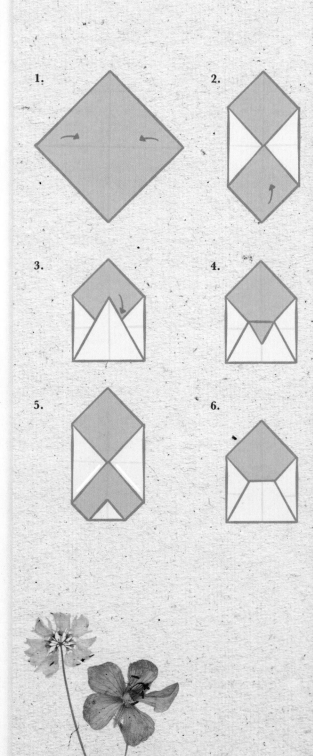

IDEAS FOR INSIDE

# ILLUSTRATED BORDERS

Borders are a wonderful addition to any spread. They can be created with cut up paper, washi tape, ribbon or lace, or good old-fashioned pen or pencil. I like to make my borders look as natural as possible, so symmetry isn't something that I particularly worry about. A lovely vine, hedgerow plants or herbs make a wonderful border so here is how to draw a border than combines all three of these elements.

**1.** First pick your medium. I've chosen watercolour and I'm going to start by sketching out my idea in pencil, so I can correct any mistakes easily. Begin with the basic border shape, drawing a line that follows the sides of the page. Let's add leaves. Leaves are pretty easy to draw, I like to create tear drop shapes with the point attached to the 'stalk'. Repeat these leaves as many times as you like. Start adding more interesting shapes such as little flowers or birds. These can be as messy or as detailed as you like. Keep working in pencil so that you can erase anything you aren't happy with, or change the positions of things.

**2.** When you have your pencilled hedgerow in place you can colour it in, starting with the leaves and plants. You can use bold colours, but I don't particularly want my border to take away from the page itself, so I've stuck to soft whimsical hues like sage and soft browns.

**3.** Continue to add colour to your pencilled illustrations. You can make berries with tiny dots of red, yellow or brown.

**4.** Once dried, the page can then be decorated further.

1.

2.

3.

4.

# TITLE WRITING IDEAS

The title of your page is usually the first thing that you read, so it needs to be visibly striking and in a good position so that you can find it quickly as you flick through your grimoire. Visually appealing titles can be achieved in many beautiful ways.

## STAMPS

Alphabet stamps come in many fonts, and I love using them for titles and short quotes. With ink pads available in lots of different colours you can achieve a wide range of looks and styles.

## SCRIPT

I find calligraphy tricky and my handwriting is barely legible, so writing titles by hand has always been a challenge, especially ones that are meant to look romantic and whimsical. The best thing I ever did was sit down to carefully and slowly trace a font I liked until muscle memory set in and now I can write a title in this style. Head on over to a font website and check out what you might like to learn.

### TYPE

Using a typewriter or printing titles out can add a neater look. This is especially useful for those who want to create their grimoire from digital assets and have a more uniformed aesthetic. You can keep fonts and themes similar throughout the book.

### COLLAGE

Using scrap paper from magazines and books to create your title needn't look like a ransom note! Cutting out and arranging words on your page can create a stunning, journal-like effect.

### PAINT

In the next few pages I am going to talk a little about creating abstract art with watercolour. The same can be done when it comes to creating titles. Making a background for your title from watercolour swatches is a great way to tie in colour and theme. When dark backgrounds are used you can write your title with white ink, which creates a stunning effect. If you want to achieve a bolder look, try swapping your watercolours for acrylic or gouache.

# WATERCOLOUR COLLAGE

As I mentioned earlier, you don't have to be an amazing artist to making amazing art. One of the easiest ways to carry this effect through to your spreads is by using abstract watercolour art. Let's look at my otter spread as an example. Apart from drawing the little otter, there was nothing to the artwork on this page. It was made using colours that I associate with the sea, rocks and seaweed; with swirled watercolours, scissors, glue and little details that I added with paint.

**1.** Start by mixing your colours. To get the shades shown I mixed forest green, burnt sienna, titanium white and yellow ochre.

**2.** Wet your watercolour paper and then gently start to dot, blend and mix your colours to create a water-like background on one half of the paper.

**3.** On the other half of the paper create the same effect with stone-like hues, and then with greens for the seaweed/kelp.

**4.** When these are dry take your paint and add little details here and there, dots and lines – nothing too ambitious, just enough to add a little depth and interest. Allow the paper to dry.

**5.** Cut out your shapes from the paper you have painted. The sea will be just a large square or rectangle to fit the majority of your page. The rocks and boulders can be various sizes, and the seaweed/kelp can be cut in long and wiggly shapes.

**6.** Start layering your cut-out pieces. Begin by gluing down your blue background. Play around with the positioning of the stones and seaweed until you're happy, and then glue them in place.

**7.** Add extra detail with coloured pencil, white gel pen or more paint. I love the effect of white writing on dark backgrounds so I copied a poem about otters in the background to help the little otter drawing stand out more. I also included a swatch of the colours I had used to add more interest.

You should be left with a sweet little three-dimensional scene that lifts itself from the page – and no fine art degree was needed! You can create lots of different collages using this technique, it's so simple yet so rewarding. You can also repeat the painting technique on more paper, cut out another shape and use it to write information on.

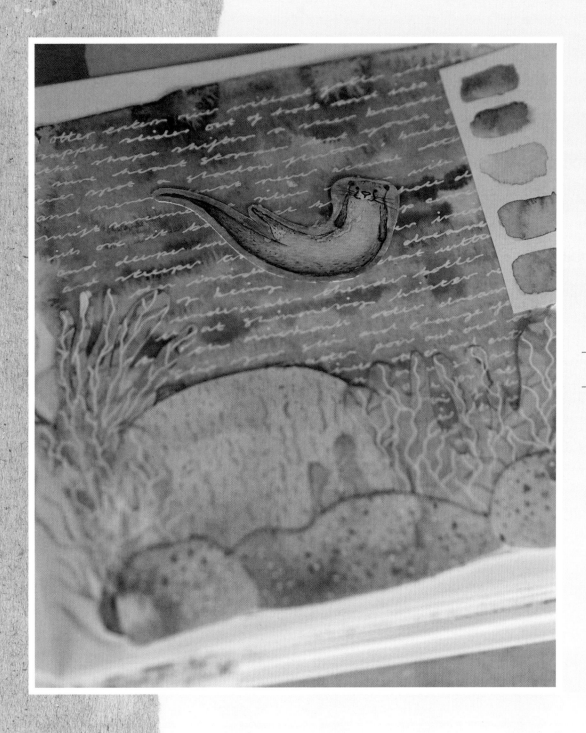

# TAG AND STAMP INSPIRATION

Making luggage tags is one of my favourite pastimes, there's just something so relaxing and satisfying about creating them. It's like having a little journal page in your hand, and adding a tag can really make your spreads pop. Tags look especially good when stamps are used, so let's make a little tag to add to our spreads.

Choose your luggage tag. They come in so many shapes and sizes, just make sure to pick one that is big enough for you to fit your chosen stamp and information on comfortably. Have a think about how you are going to decorate it, and what sort of information you want on it. Once you've decided, assemble your things and start with your first layer.

**1.** If you have chosen a paper background, begin by sticking that to the tag. I like to use pages from books because they're usually quite thin and stamp ink takes to them well.

**2.** Take your stamp and press it carefully where you want it on your tag. I like to avoid positioning design elements too centrally, it looks more interesting to angle things or to use only half the stamp on the tag.

**3.** Add any extras such as washi tape or stickers. If you are going to add writing or a title to the tag, consider how much space you need for this and keep stickers out of this area. It's almost impossible to write on most sticker paper without the ink smudging, so try to avoid that if you can. Add any writing and finish the tag with a ribbon or yarn through the hole at the top.

The layers and different textures combined in a small space should look really interesting and detailed, so that your tag will add so much to its chosen spread.

1.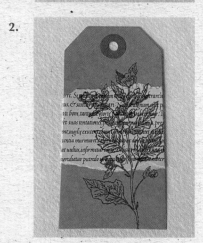

2.

3.

# WHEEL OF THE YEAR SPINNER

The Wheel of the Year is an amazing thing to celebrate, so creating a wonderful spread that encapsulates all the feelings of the passing seasons is a tough gig: how can you fit so much onto one page? This idea, using split pins, is great fun. It allows you to turn the two-dimensional into something that can be interacted with. Let's see how we can use it on our Wheel of the Year spread…

**1.** Take some thick paper – watercolour is good – and using a compass or something circular, draw a circle about a third of the size of your grimoire's pages.

**2.** With a ruler draw lines until you have eight equal sections, each line will need to be at a 45-degree angle to the previous one. These sections will represent each of the festivals of the year.

**3.** Decorate each section with that festival's aesthetic in mind. You can draw small scenes like I did, or you can use stamps, washi tape, stickers or anything else that takes your fancy. I used coloured pencils and gold pen to really make my wheel stand out from the page.

**4.** Once you are happy with your wheel's décor, cut it out. Go to the page it will be stuck to and decorate it however you like. At the top I like to make a little header that says 'currently', when your wheel turns the ongoing festival will be at the top.

1.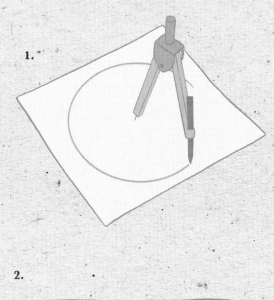

2.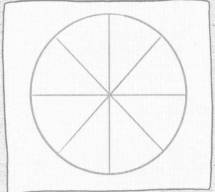

**5.**

**5.** Poke a hole in the centre of your wheel and in the centre of your page. Take a split pin and poke it through both the circle and the page, making sure the wheel can turn fully without ripping the paper. Open out the back of the split pin to secure it in place.

**6.** Glue the blank page behind this spread to hide the back of the split pin.

This idea doesn't have to be constrained to just this project, you can use it for a multitude of things, like Sigils and spell ingredients. Making it interactive helps you to retain the information that this feature contains, and is much more enjoyable to use.

# SIGILS

Sigils are symbols created by witches and other spiritual practitioners to invoke, protect, attract or banish. They have been used for hundreds of years by a variety of cultures and religions and have appeared everywhere from the columns of Egyptian burial chambers to the wooden mantles of medieval fireplaces.

These symbols may look like a bunch of swirls and dots but they are incredibly useful for so many aspects of your craft. Sigils are traditionally drawn on paper, using ink, paint or even ash, but they can be used anywhere in any form. Sigils can be drawn in the air using the smoke from incense to protect a space or a ritual; they can be painted onto windows using water to attract good luck to the home; or they can be drawn in the sand and taken by the tide to let go of any unwanted feelings we are hanging on to.

52

**1.**

**2.**

**3.**

# Simple alphabet circle sigil

Sigils look sort of complicated and a little daunting to beginners, and there are many ways that people choose to create them. I've found that the easiest and most efficient way for myself is to create an alphabet circle.

**1.** Write the alphabet out in a circle. You can choose to do it in order, or you can choose to randomise the letters, do whatever you feel called to on the day.

Write a sentence about what you would like your sigil to do for you, for example…

'Success comes easily to me'

Take each letter only once, write them down in the order they appear like this:

S u c e o m a i l y t

**2.** Starting from the first letter, join them in order with a pen or pencil until you are left with a shape.

**3.** Copy the shape out again, place a dot at the start and at the end of the line. This is your finished sigil.

You can keep this basic shape, or you can add some artistic flare to it, by adding leaves or further swirls and shapes. Colour is often used to add an extra layer of energy to a sigil. You can use green to invoke prosperity, yellow for creativity, orange for joy etc. It's entirely up to your intuition how you bring this sigil to life.

If you're having a little trouble creating your own sigils, the following pages contain some examples and ideas that you can use in your grimoire to get you started…

53

## Grimoire protection sigil

'Protection' is a very broad term in witchcraft and it's often thrown around casually on social media without much investigation. What exactly will we be protecting our grimoire from?

This protection sigil covers a lot of bases:

**Spiritual Protection** We are making sure that no negative energies or influencing energies from other witches enter the pages. Remember that a grimoire is a working tool and therefore is susceptible to psychic attack and syphoning of energy.

**Physical Protection** Although it's a spiritual tool, a grimoire is very much a physical object, so of course will be at the mercy of the elements. You can protect it from misadventure such as fire, water and general wear and tear… but remember that it's important to store your grimoire safely, a sigil can only do so much.

54

*'Protect this grimoire'*

## Attracting creativity

It is ironic that we creative people often struggle with keeping hold of our creative spark. Creativity is almost a sentient thing, a companion that we need to keep fed and watered, and warm and comfortable. When we neglect it, it seems to wander and then eventually leave… so this sigil is great to keep the creative spark burning within.

*'One with creativity'*

## Motivation

I find I go through stages of motivation. Sometimes I am overflowing with ideas and feel like I'll never stop creating. Then comes a period of stagnancy where no matter how hard I try the energy is unaligned and I can't bring myself to pick up a paintbrush. Of course we should take breaks when we need to – avoiding burnout is important – but sometimes we want to create so badly but cannot find the motivation. That's where this sigil comes in…

*'I am energised'*

## Charging your sigil

To charge a sigil is to breathe life into it using your own energy. I like to draw the sigil and place it on my charging station – a small slice of wood with an animal painted on it. The animal I choose depends on what my sigil is for. I might select the barn owl to charge the sigil 'one with creativity' to invoke the wisdom that owls symbolise. You don't have to charge a sigil this way, you can cleanse it with incense and meditate with it for a while. Or you can create a crystal grid, a rune circle, or invoke the elements using symbols. It all depends on what you resonate with. My sigil sits on its charging station, I light a candle and some incense, play some music and sit with the sigil, thinking deeply about what I want it to do for me. I envision a future in which it is working and the words it is made from are manifested.

Sigils are incredibly versatile and one way to include them within your grimoire is to write them on paper and burn them with dried herbs (chosen to reflect your intention), and then to mix a little of the ash with the paint you are using. This adds a deeper connection with your creative spirit and takes your artwork from the mundane to the magickal. Try keeping a separate notebook for your sigils. Whenever you create a new one, draw it in the book and keep it safe for the next time you need to use it.

# RITUALS

Rituals make up a large part of my craft, from self-love bathing rituals involving candles and homemade bath salts, to year-long manifestation rituals. As your grimoire sits on your altar it will absorb something of the rituals and spells that you do, so it's a good idea to keep it cleansed if you don't want certain energies to linger. Cleansing your grimoire can be as simple as using intentions and wafting incense over it and between the pages, or you can use sound, or leave it by a window to bathe in moonlight during various phases. Keeping it cleansed means it can remain a positive tool in your witchy arsenal, and through ritual we can turn your grimoire from the mundane into the magickal…

## Ritual one: A new season

The Wheel of the Year has turned once more, and we find ourselves in a brand new season. Usually at the altar we change up imagery and add different plants and objects to commemorate the new energy. How can we include the grimoire? A wonderful way to keep track of the festivals and remind yourself of their energy in your grimoire is to create an energetically aligning bookmark.

### You will need

- Your chosen notebook/journal
- A bookmark-sized piece of card
- Creative supplies (paper, string, paint)
- Smoke (incense, dried sage/rosemary, herbal blend)
- Sound (relaxing music, bells, sound bowls)
- A homemade sigil that invokes the feeling of the festival (see Sigils)

## METHOD

This is a creative ritual, one that focuses the mind via gentle concentration. The creation of these seasonal bookmarks means that you will be left with several you can rotate for use in your grimoire throughout the year.

Let's create a bookmark for the festival of Mabon:

**1.** Start by gathering your creative supplies and making yourself comfortable before lighting incense or playing music. Set your ritual up to make you feel relaxed and ready to create.

**2.** Calling upon your inner magpie (see Cultivating a Magpie Mind), lay out the paper, string or paints that you want to use to create your little Mabon scene.

**3.** Think about your favourite things about this festival and allow yourself the freedom to create freely and without judgement.

**4.** Add your sigil. This doesn't have to be on view, it can be discretely placed on the back of the bookmark.

**5.** Finish by cleansing your bookmark, tools and space.

Think about where you might like to store your bookmarks when they aren't being used. A pencil case, or a box in which you can also add a couple of crystals to keep them cleansed would more than suffice. Take out each bookmark as you need it and allow it to move and flow through your grimoire as you do.

# Ritual two: Good morning grimoire

I like to carve out time in the morning a couple of times a week in order to create a page in my grimoire. There's just something about the start of a new day – the quiet expectation and the energy in the air makes for a magickal time. All the more reason for you to use it to do a peaceful morning ritual to help you bond with your grimoire and welcome a new day…

## You will need

- Your grimoire, open on a page set aside with a place to store daily readings. I have created a spread with an envelope (see Ideas for Inside) to pop in my little bits of paper
- A warm drink (I love lavender, chamomile and honey in the morning)
- Your preferred way of cleansing (smoke, sound etc, this morning I am going to be using some incense meant to attract positive vibes)
- A tarot or oracle deck
- Paper and pen

## METHOD

**1.** First cleanse your space, yourself and your grimoire. You've spent a whole night sleeping, dreaming and balancing on the threads of the thin veil that separates this world from the next, so cleansing before a morning ritual is important – it's like taking a spiritual shower.

**2.** Sit quietly for a while with your tea and your card deck. Enjoy the silence of your surroundings or listen to the quiet hums and tones that may be happening around you. Whilst sitting with your cards and your grimoire ask for a message, a card of the day, to help guide you in your choices and decision making.

**3.** Draw a card and spend some time thinking about its meaning. While drinking your tea, write down whatever comes to mind, trying not to take a pause in thought. Let your thoughts flow with the ink onto your paper. Allow your brain to empty itself of its ideas and interpretations of the card that has shown itself to you.

**4.** Cleanse your paper and then pop it into the spread dedicated to your daily readings. Your thoughts will merge with the energy of the grimoire throughout the day, taking on your spiritual messages and allowing you the headspace to carry on with your day.

The real crime is art
remaining unseen
and unloved

# CULTIVATING A MAGPIE MIND

As a witch, you will most likely have a fondness and an attraction for trinkets and curiosities. You'll feel drawn to the cluttered corners of charity shops where the perfect-but-chipped ceramic dish awaits, the dusty corridors of second-hand bookstores that contain illustrations perfect for your altar wall, and the thick undergrowth of the hedgerow where the forgotten bones of wildlife lie waiting to be collected.

Channelling your inner magpie is vital for creating a grimoire that reflects who you are as a witch and as a person. Of course there are lots of lovely mass-produced stickers and ephemera available to buy online, but there is such joy to be had from the physical gathering of pre-loved supplies. It is the mindful act of seeking, obtaining and recycling that adds an extra layer of energy to your magickal tome.

So how do we apply this magpie state of mind to the creation of our grimoire? Rather than rushing to the shops and breaking the bank buying expensive papers, fabrics and stickers, take the time to have a leisurely stroll around your home and see what you can gather. An old picture book, a magazine, the greetings card that's been pinned to your noticeboard for months, an empty seed packet… all these forgotten and unused items hold creative potential. As a curious collector you should seek out the creative potential in everything. Gathering supplies from your home not only fills your craft cupboard but also gets rid of clutter and rubbish in your space. Of course, if you wish you can splash out on more luxury items, fancy paper and decorated envelopes, but there are treasures to be found in the forgotten things in drawers and cupboards.

## What sort of treasures are we on the hunt for?

Cards, thread, ribbon, wrapping paper, gift tags, book pages, music sheets… there is so much we can use when it comes to decorating our grimoires that we're spoiled for choice!

Don't just seek out paper goods as you can fit so much more into your grimoire décor-wise. Keep an eye out for ribbons, threads and strings from gift-wrap as well as just keeping the paper. Visit your local DIY store, pick up some free paint swatches and cut shapes and tags from them. Head to antiques stores to see if they stock old photos and postcards that you can use to layer your backgrounds with. The same goes for sheet music – there is something magickal about including songs on pages, to add deeper meaning.

Fabric is another decorative element you can take advantage of. Do you have a blouse that you love the pattern on, but can't wear anymore? Cut strips from it to use as borders or as ribbons for tags. In the same way, fabric squares make wonderful backgrounds and add a delightful textured element to your pages.

Ask friends if they have books they no longer want, and use the text pages as backgrounds, or cut out and arrange words into sentences for intrigue. Seek to repurpose the art from old calendars and planners rather than throwing them away. Create your own papers by using coffee- and tea-staining techniques.

Papermaking is relatively easy when you have the correct tools, and there are myriad techniques and tips available to us via clever creatives and their online video tutorials. Dried flowers can be added to paper pulp – the result is just so beautiful. Depending on the flowers and herbs used, papers like these can add further magick and intent to the pages. Some may find the idea of tearing pages from an old book horrifying, or cutting images from them an unforgiveable crime, but I much prefer the idea that instead of languishing on a dusty shelf, or in a box in a charity shop, these pages and pictures get a second life as part of a page in a magickal book. The real crime is art remaining unseen and unloved. Your grimoire is in constant use, so you will see and appreciate these decorative elements repeatedly – far more than you would have done if they'd stayed in their original form.

This thrifty attitude is rewarding, and the benefits are clear when you see your collection growing. However, that doesn't mean that having magpie tendencies means you must hoard everything you come across. Magpies are smart, they observe their surroundings and pick things carefully. If you've ever seen a magpie hop around a bottle cap, tilt its head and survey it closely before carrying it away (or leaving it), you'll know that there is an obvious process of critical thought involved.

## Considerations for magpies

### 1. DO I LIKE IT?

Do you find it visibly attractive? Does it fit with your aesthetic/colour scheme/theme that you have picked for your grimoire?

### 2. WILL I USE IT?

Of course you may have other projects that you want to try that you can use this item for, but have you got an idea for it in mind already? Avoid grabbing it just for the sake of having it.

### 3. WILL IT WORK?

Physically, is it a material that you can work with? I'm guilty of trying to stick pressed flowers into my grimoire, only for the delicate petals to disintegrate upon closing and opening the pages. Keep in mind the kind of traffic your grimoire is going to experience and bear that in mind when you pick your decorative materials.

62

## Keep track of your supplies

Acknowledge your limitations in terms of space or storage. Not everyone has a dedicated room in which to store all their delightful finds. Don't chuck everything into a teetering pile on your dining table and risk a feeling of overwhelm. It is important to use up the supplies you already have, and having a good system of stock rotation is key. I've been guilty of acting like Tolkein's dragon Smaug atop a glittering pile of coveted stickers, but these things are meant to be used and enjoyed, and to be turned into art.

If you find yourself with too many supplies, it may be time to have a good sort out. Lay everything out, look at what you have and what inspires you. You'll find that seeing everything together will spur you to create a spread you may not have thought of whilst everything was piled up or shut away in drawers.

Storage is key and I love the large wooden box that I use to store all my paper scraps and clippings. It's a wonderful feeling to delve into that treasure chest and pull forgotten scraps from the bottom of it, or to add some more. Stickers do well stored in folders, as do bits of ephemera. I roll ribbons around pegs, clipping them in place, and keep bits of fabric tumbled together in storage boxes where, like all my supplies, they await their turn in the grimoire.

You can also become a digital magpie and head to the internet to find a wonderful array of illustrations and ephemera. Just bear in mind where you are sourcing these images. Pinterest, the image-sharing platform, is such a brilliant website to get inspiration from, but taking images from there often means that artists go uncredited. Images on Pinterest boards often come from secondary sites where the art has been stolen. Instead, stick to public domain or royalty-free image sites such as Unsplash. Or you could use subscription sites such as Canva and RawPixel, where you can find thousands of pictures, photos and graphics to use in your private journalling. Printing out images that catch your eye means you will soon have a lot to choose from, all for just the cost of a subscription.

Being a magickal magpie is as rewarding as it is practical, and with our focus turned towards helping our beloved planet, it makes sense to repurpose and recycle where we can. The hunt for beautiful and practical decoration is as fun and worthwhile as the decorating process itself. It is worth remembering that your grimoire is your own and it is entirely up to you how you adorn it. Not everything has to have meaning, not everything has to be thrifted, but it *should* reflect your craft – that will be the easiest part of the process.

63

# INSPIRATION – WHERE TO FIND IT

## Style with meaning

As a Taurus sun, I am a cheerleader for everything sumptuous, aesthetic and decorative, so it's no secret that everything I do has beauty at the fore. From time to time I have received comments and messages online where the stylistic choices of my grimoire have come into question – I am asked how much of my online presence is 'aesthetic' and how much of it is 'real'.

It is a valid and important question to contemplate.

### THE QUESTION OF AESTHETICS

With the rise in witchcraft and alternative spiritual ideas in general, the question has been raised as to how many young people are turning to witchcraft simply because they like the 'witchy aesthetic' and enjoy replicating it in their social media. Of course, it is not up to others to dictate how people live their lives and what they take enjoyment from, especially when it comes to creativity and spirituality, but there is a certain phrase I state when people question my dedication to my craft versus how I present it online:

*'Witchcraft isn't an aesthetic, but an aesthetic can be witchcraft.'*

Witchcraft, at its core, is a practitioner's symbiotic relationship with nature, how they work with the physical and spiritual energies of the earth and universe,

to heal, manifest or solve a problem, and live the life of their dreams. You do not need to have a stunningly decorated altar, or a grimoire heaving with luxury stationery, in order to be a witch.

That being said, I do take a lot of power and energy from my space. There is nothing in my grimoire or on the walls of my altar that does not hold meaning or isn't there to serve a purpose. I take joy from my spaces when they are filled with drying herbs and flowers. I infuse them with the scent of incense and sounds of my sacred space. When I place a picture of a kingfisher on my altar wall, I am reminded that patience and hard work produce rewards. The pale pink string I use to tie tags to my grimoire isn't just pretty, its colour prompts feelings of serenity and calm, just the right touch for a page about a self-love ritual.

### YOUR MAGIC, YOUR STYLE

To reduce an elaborate-looking practice to 'just an aesthetic' does a disservice to all the thought, knowledge (and energy) that goes into creating these spaces and places. This kind of visual practice may not be for you, you may just need an altar cloth and a candle in order to do your magick, but it is *your* magick. If other styles don't work for you then that's fine and it doesn't lessen your experience in any way.

I find power in my aesthetic, solace in the calming energy of my crystals and animal bones, delight in my pressed flowers, and motivation in the art that adorns my grimoire. There is inspiration to be found everywhere.

to do

But, soft! what light through yonder window
    breaks?
It is the east, and Juliet is the sun!—
Arise, fair sun, and kill the envious moon,
Who is already sick and pale with grief,
That thou her maid art far more fair than she:

Spells

By accident most strange
Now my dear lady
Brought to the
I find my
A most au
If now I c
Will ever
Thou art
And giv

VINTAGE
STAMP
HAND ACCOUNT
B.T.C 1980

RETURN
TICKET 12/-
Amberley to Brisbane

Sage

MOONLIT SPELLS
EX-LIBRIS

W

Be open to
the universe

WINSOR & NEWTON    WINSOR & NEWTO    WINSOR & NEWTON    WINSOR & NEWTO    WINSOR & NEWTON

## Inspired by nature

When it comes to decorating a grimoire we need look no further for inspiration than nature herself…

**TAKE YOUR SENSES OUTSIDE**

On an early autumn walk you can stand and take note of the traffic-light hues of leaves turning from green to amber to red. You can find opposite colours that complement each other in summer wildflower meadows, such as blue cornflowers and crimson poppies. The striking patterns in shells and feathers, the symmetry of butterflies and the rough stripes of tree bark give us ideas about how to use texture alongside colour.

When I am in a creative rut, I find that the best way to shake those feelings is to walk in nature and really pay attention to what is going on around you as you never know when inspiration will strike. Even in winter, when everything seems stark, lifeless and grey, you will find ideas in the scratchy, hessian-like textures of the landscape, in the skeletal arms of trees and the empty seed pods encased in glittering frost.

Bring nature home with you and lay it out on your altar. A nature table of flowers, abandoned nests, moss and herbs will help you decide what sort of page you want to create that day. Studying these finds either through sketching or painting will help you hone the creative skills that you want to bring to your grimoire.

## SEEK OUT ART THAT INSPIRES YOU

Find inspiration in art itself with a trip to a gallery or by searching for pictures on the internet. I'm inspired by the art of John William Waterhouse, whose works include wood nymphs, women from ancient history and myth, and sumptuous nature scenes. Beatrix Potter's watercolours feature all the earthy and spring-like hues and tones that I like to dress my altar in. Jackie Morris and her wonderfully whimsical animals have a special place in my heart, and her use of soft lines and contrasting bold colours remind me that I can be both soft and strong in the way that I create my spreads.

## CHANNEL YOUR INNER CHILD

At the centre of this style of journalling is a desire to replicate the carefree playtime that I enjoyed as an art-loving child. My biggest inspiration comes from a childhood spent painting, drawing and creating models. There are wonderful feelings associated with the memory of experiencing things for the first time as a child – experimenting without fear of failure, ridicule or the concern of making a mess or a mistake.

As adults we are guarded when it comes to creativity, and this can come across in the way that we go about using our supplies. How freeing it is to just tip out all your pencils as you once did as a child! It may seem messy and pointless but in the jumble of pencils you'll find colours laid next to each other that you may not have thought about using. When you mix paint without the worry that you are wasting it, you discover the perfect lavender colour, or just the right shade of brown that you were looking for to paint the flecks on a kestrel's wing.

Stamping, cutting, gluing and sticking, scribbling and splattering are all worthy artistic activities that needn't be left in the child's bedroom that sits at the back of your mind. Invite that inner child to play and learn how much joy can be involved in creating.

67

Witchcraft,
at its heart,
is all about
getting creative

# AFTERWORD

I hope you're inspired and excited to create your own grimoire. The papers that follow have been lovingly assembled for you to make envelopes, borders, backgrounds and pockets from, but don't limit your creativity to the things here. Witchcraft, at its heart, is all about getting creative; it's about bringing forth energies from within and around us, and shaping them. Your imagination and instincts are the best guides on this spiritual journey, but more than anything this part of your craft is about self-love. From imposter syndrome to low self-esteem, there are many 'road blocks' to a creative life. You may fear being judged, you may have had a bad experience when you shared your creative side, and so you might feel reserved when creating your grimoire. But it doesn't do to live in the shadows when there's a beautiful creative sun shining in your life.

## A spell for creative confidence

So here's a spell – specially crafted for you, dear reader – to bolster the creative confidence that I hope this book has sparked inside you…

### You will need

- Rose/lavender incense
- Two bags of tea containing chamomile/rose/lavender, one to drink and one to use as ingredients
- Tarot cards: Temperance for patience, The Empress for confidence, Ace of Cups for compassion
- Small cotton bag
- Dried flowers/herbs: pink rosebuds (for self-love), elderflower (for transition and creative joy), chamomile (for calm in self), juniper berries (for regeneration and hope), lavender (for happiness and peaceful love)

## METHOD

**1.** Start by making yourself comfortable: cleanse your space, play music or do whatever it is you like to do when you are creating a spell; then make up one of the bags of tea into a warm drink.

**2.** Put all the remaining ingredients (except the elderflower) into a bowl, or a cauldron, adding the contents of the second bag of tea (identical to the one that you are drinking) so that the ingredients in the spell mirror what you are physically consuming.

**3.** Cleanse the mix with your incense.

**4.** As you drink your tea, place the three tarot cards in front of you and think about their message and how it applies to you. Think about your relationship with yourself, your creativity and your vulnerability, and acknowledge any hard feelings you have.

**5.** Put everything into the little bag then add the elderflower at the end to symbolise the transition from self-doubt to self-love.

**6.** Lastly, cleanse the finished bag with the rest of the incense and hang it where you create – this might be your altar, an office, a desk etc – or keep it on your person for one week.

The ritual is finished when the incense has burned down, and you have finished drinking your tea.

This spell is a great kick-starter to the spiritual work that you can do to help you stay on your creative path. Just like witchcraft, creativity is something that you never stop learning about. There is always something to investigate, to try, to learn from.

*Keep a curious and open mind, and remember that the act of making art is the most magical act of all.*

# PAPERS

I am absolutely thrilled to be able to include some gorgeous papers in this book for you to use in your own grimoire. These have been designed and chosen to inspire creativity and give you a good starting point for decorating your spreads.

In the next half of this book, you will find papers that take inspiration from the beauty of nature – leaves, flowers and textures that will bring the outside in to the pages of your grimoire (without the mud). There are a range of colours, shades and hues to select from so that you can create with intention. Some designs are bold and are made to take centre stage on the page, others are muted and happy to serve as the background for your own unique design ideas. Match colours with intentions, illustrations with ingredients and textures with aesthetic.

When I flicked through these papers I was especially thrilled with the borders. I felt inspired to create a 'paper apothecary'. I drew a load of small spell bottles in my grimoire, including drawings of herbs inside them, before taking the frames from this book's papers, gluing them to tags, writing the ingredients and then tying them to the bottles with twine. The papers will also make wonderful envelopes, like the ones we talked about in the Ideas for Inside section of this book, or tags or bookmarks. The only limit is your imagination.

I would encourage you to not be too precious with this part of the book. Rip and tear, slice and snip to your heart's desire and when you find your supply dwindling take inspiration from what you have used and recreate the illustrations, borders and patterns in your own way. Save the offcuts from the papers and create a collage similar to the watercolour collage spread earlier in this book, or tear them up, turn them into pulp and use them to create your own papers. Take this as your sign to branch out into new creative pursuits and learn new crafting skills.

One of my favourite things to do with a beautifully illustrated or designed book (when I have finished reading it, and re-reading if I wished to) is to flick through and take out pages that appeal to me to use in journalling. From illustrations I love to patterned endpapers, they are all wonderful assets for journalling and for cultivating the magpie mind that I have talked about. I would urge that when you are done with this book, you take what you like and use it in your grimoires and journals. It may seem scary and sacrilegious to cut up a book, but I believe that a life spent gathering dust on a shelf is a much worse fate for *The Handmade Grimoire*!

Printable versions of these papers can also be downloaded from www.davidandcharles.com.

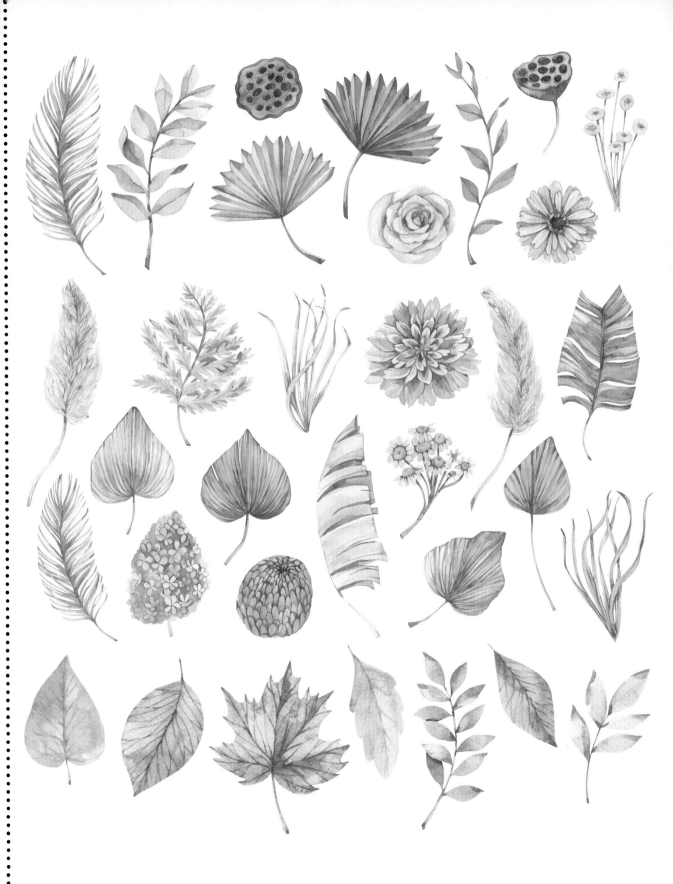

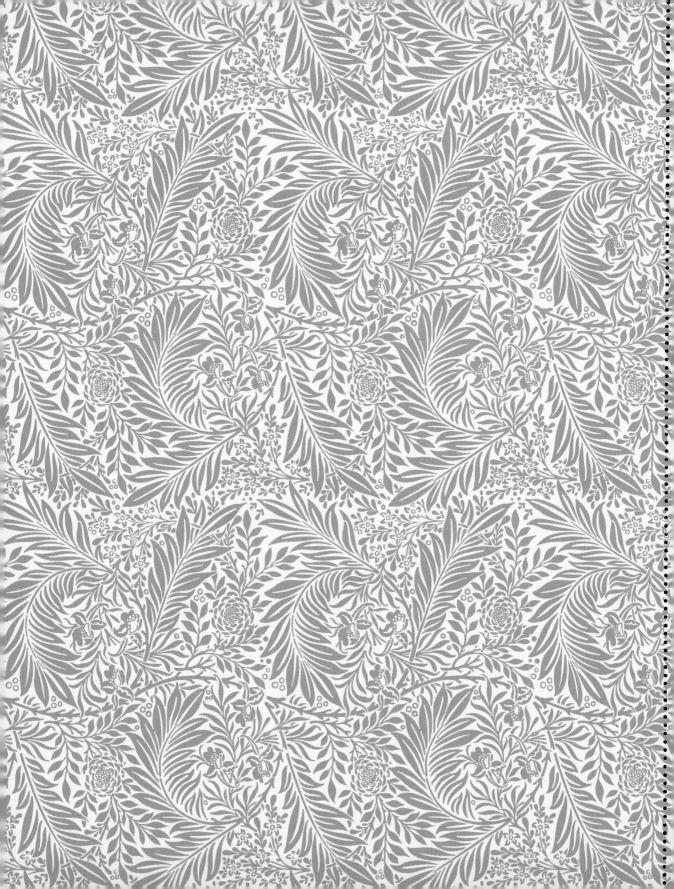

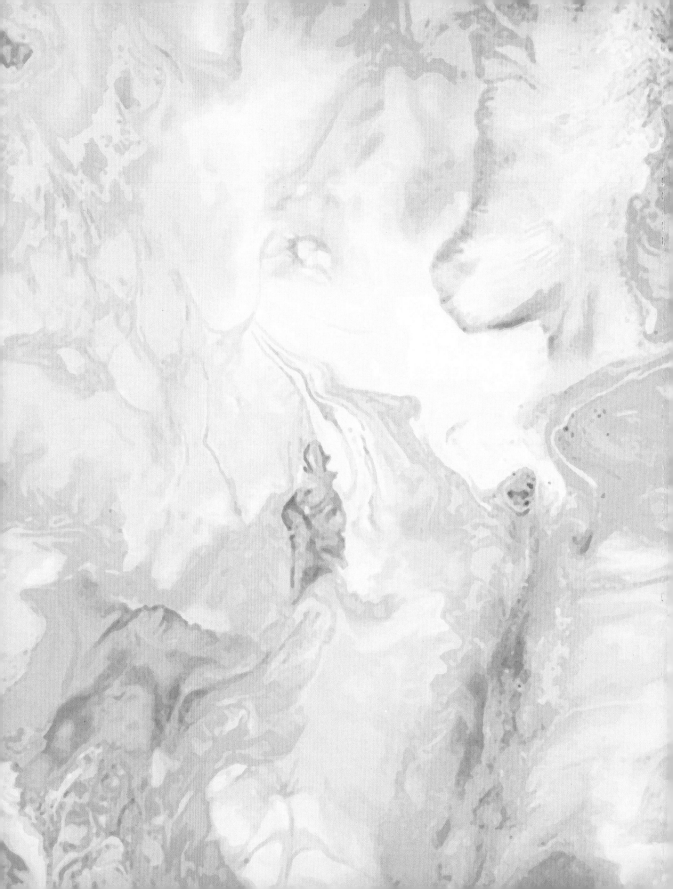

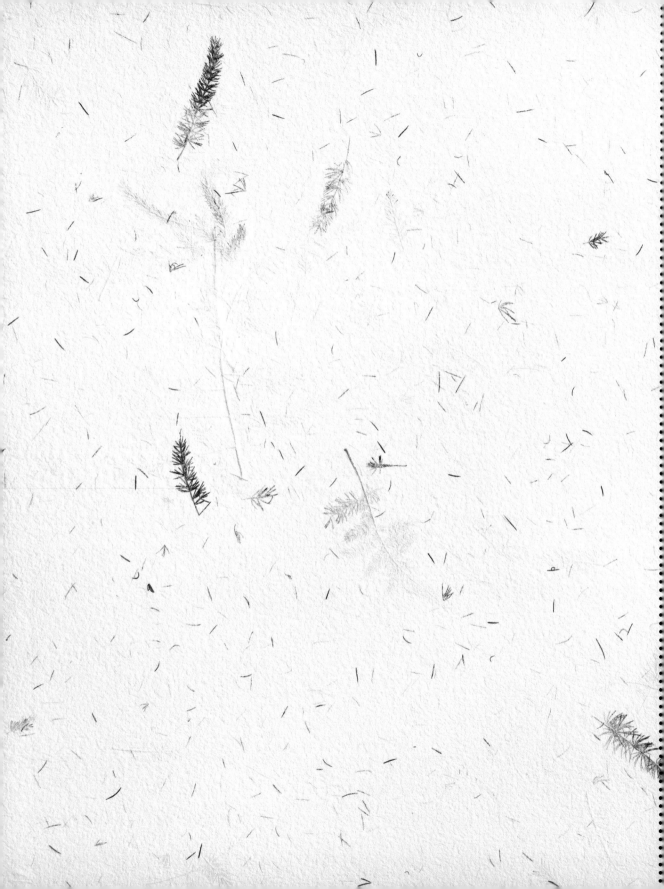

# ACKNOWLEDGEMENTS

The immense enjoyment I have gotten from writing this book would not have been felt were it not for the following amazing humans:

Lizzie, my book-midwife, thank you for your trust and for your expertise and for being just as excited about stationery as I am. You made this entire process a breeze during a stormy time, and I am so glad to have worked with you.

To the team at David and Charles, thank you for bringing my aesthetic to these pages, for listening to my thoughts and most of all for the opportunity to create this beautiful book.

To my amazing friends and followers on social media – your support means the world to me and I feel so lucky that we can create magickal things together. I'm so excited to have you along for this journey, one I would not be on were it not for your support.

My family, thank you for being my biggest cheerleaders. Huge thanks to my Mum who took the reins of my household for a few months and made sure I had nothing to do but create this book.

To Dad, you encouraged me to write more than anyone. I just wish you could have held this book in your hands, you would have been so thrilled to read it.

Nahla, thank you for not using all of Mummy's best art supplies during this process, it is much appreciated.

Last but by no means least, an enormous thank you to my fantastic husband Simon, whose unquestioning and steadfast belief in me means I have the confidence and support to pursue my dreams.

142

# SUPPLIERS

**PAINTS & INKS**

Winsor & Newton – www.winsornewton.com/uk

**STAMPS, WASHI TAPE & PAPERS**

Craft Consortium – www.craftconsortium.com
Notebook Therapy – www.notebooktherapy.com
Washi Tape – www.thewashitapeshop.com

**PENS**

Tombow – www.tombow.co.uk
Sakura – www.sakuraofamerica.com
Zebra – www.zebrapen.com
Archer & Olive – www.archerandolive.com

**STICKERS**

John Derian – www.johnderian.com

# ABOUT THE AUTHOR

Laura Derbyshire is a writer, artist and hedge witch who lives in Oxfordshire with her husband and daughter. She has been a witch for over a decade and a devotee of all things nature and art-related for much longer. Laura incorporates nature-centred magick into her daily life and encourages creatives to mix art with spirituality, the mundane with the magickal, and to find joy in all that nature has to offer.

Laura first started sharing her grimoires on social media during the pandemic lockdown of winter 2020, and has since amassed a dedicated following of like-minded people wanting to bring their journals to life and sprinkle a little magick into their everyday journalling routine.

*The Handmade Grimoire* is Laura's debut book.

# INDEX

A DAVID AND CHARLES BOOK
© David and Charles, Ltd 2023

David and Charles is an imprint of David and Charles, Ltd
Suite A, Tourism House, Pynes Hill, Exeter, EX2 5WS

Text and Designs © Laura Derbyshire 2023
Layout and Photography © David and Charles, Ltd 2023

First published in the UK and USA in 2023

A catalogue record for this book is available from the
British Library.

ISBN-13: 9781446309681 paperback
ISBN-13: 9781446312735 EPUB
ISBN-13: 9781446312742 PDF

This book has been printed on paper from approved
suppliers and made from pulp from sustainable sources.

Printed in China through Asia Pacific Offset for:
David and Charles, Ltd
Suite A, Tourism House, Pynes Hill, Exeter, EX2 5WS

10 9 8 7 6 5 4 3 2 1

Publishing Director: Ame Verso
Senior Commissioning Editor: Lizzie Kaye
Managing Editor: Jeni Chown
Copy Editor: Jane Trollope
Head of Design: Anna Wade
Designers: Sam Staddon and Lee-May Lim
Photography: Laura Derbyshire
Pre-press Designer: Ali Stark
Production Manager: Beverley Richardson

David and Charles publishes high-quality books on
a wide range of subjects. For more information visit
www.davidandcharles.com.

Share your stories with us on social media using
#dandcbooks and follow us on Facebook and
Instagram by searching for @dandcbooks.

Layout of the digital edition of this book may vary
depending on reader hardware and display settings.